The
Christmas
Play

For Richard Baker
and all my friends at the Bracknell Drama Club,
with love and thanks C.B.

For Rebecca J.P.

Text copyright © 1996 Clare Bevan
Illustrations copyright © 1999 Julie Park
This edition copyright © 1999 Lion Publishing

The moral rights of the author and illustrator
have been asserted

Published by
Lion Publishing plc
Sandy Lane West, Oxford, England
www.lion-publishing.co.uk
ISBN 0 7459 3990 2

First edition 1999
10 9 8 7 6 5 4 3 2 1 0

This poem first appeared in *Star of Wonder*,
published by Lion Publishing plc, 1996

A catalogue record for this book is available
from the British Library

Typeset in 28/32 Kidprint MT
Printed and bound in Singapore

The Christmas Play

Clare Bevan

Illustrations by Julie Park

LION
Children's Books

Here is an inn with a stable,
Equipped with some straw and a chair.
Here is an angel in bed sheets,
With tinsel to tie back her hair.

Here is a servant in bath towels,
Who sweeps round the stage with a broom.
Here is a chorus of faces,
All eager to cry out, 'NO ROOM!'

Here is a Joseph who stammers,
And tries to remember his lines.
Here is a teacher in anguish,
Who frantically gestures and signs.

Here is 'Away In A Manger'—
A tune MOST recorders can play.
Here is the moment of wonder,
As Jesus appears in the hay.

Here is a Mary with freckles,
Whose baby is plastic and hard.
Here is a donkey in trousers,
With ears made from pieces of card.

Here is a shepherd in curtains,
Who carries a crook made of wire.
Here is a boy sucking cough sweets,
Who growls from the back of the choir.

While shepherds watched their flocks by night...

Here is a King bearing bath salts,
Who points at a star hung on strings.
Here is a dove who has stage fright,
And quivers her crêpe-paper wings.

Here is a page boy in slippers,
Who stumbles his way up the stairs.
Here is a long line of cherubs,
Who march round the manger in pairs.

Here is a camel who fidgets,
With plasters stuck over his knee.
Here are some sheep who
    just giggle,
And think no one out there can see.

Ssshhh!

Here is a Herod in glasses,
Who whispers, so nobody hears.
Here is a Mum with a hanky,
To cover her pride and her tears.

Here is our final production,
And though it's still held up with pins,
The parents will love every minute—
For this is where Christmas begins.